Magoon, Kekla.

BIO   **The Zebulon Pike**
PIK   **expedition**

DATE DUE

The Zebulon Pike Expedition

Kekla Magoon
AR B.L.: 7.3 Alt.: 1102
Points: 2.0   MG

THE ZEBULON PIKE
EXPEDITION

Essential Events

THE ZEBULON PIKE
EXPEDITION
BY KEKLA MAGOON

Content Consultant
Matt Mayberry
Director, Colorado Springs Museum

ABDO
Publishing Company

CREDITS

Published by ABDO Publishing Company, 8000 West 78th Street,
Edina, Minnesota 55439. Copyright © 2009 by Abdo Consulting
Group, Inc. International copyrights reserved in all countries. No
part of this book may be reproduced in any form without written
permission from the publisher. The Essential Library™ is a
trademark and logo of ABDO Publishing Company.

Printed in the United States.

Editor: Abby DeBruine
Copy Editor: Paula Lewis
Interior Design and Production: Emily Love
Cover Design: Emily Love

Library of Congress Cataloging-in-Publication Data
Magoon, Kekla.
  The Zebulon Pike expedition / by Kekla Magoon.
     p. cm. — (Essential events)
  Includes bibliographical references and index.
  ISBN 978-1-60453-518-1
  1. Pike, Zebulon Montgomery, 1779-1813—Juvenile literature.
2. Explorers—West (U.S.)—Biography—Juvenile literature. 3.
West (U.S.)—Discovery and exploration—Juvenile literature. 4.
Southwest, New—Discovery and exploration—Juvenile literature. 5.
West (U.S.)—History—To 1848—Juvenile literature. 6. Southwest,
New—History—To 1848—Juvenile literature. I. Title.

  F592.P653M34 2009
  917.804'2092—dc22
  [B]

                          2008033109

TABLE OF CONTENTS

Sangre de Cristo Mountains

LOST

The air was bone-chilling, and the snow was waist deep. There were more men than horses and not enough food and blankets to go around. The men were not wearing warm clothing, and many of them had to walk across the frozen ground without suitable shoes. This small group of explorers crossed the Sangre de Cristo Mountains in present-day Colorado during the winter of 1807. Now they were lost, and their path had taken them into territory where they did not belong.

Their leader, Zebulon Montgomery Pike, was a 28-year-old lieutenant in the U.S. Army. Following the course of a river southward, Pike marched his team into the cold and snow. The men were cold, hungry, and tired, and their spirits sagged, but Pike was a man on a mission.

Too Cold to Continue

As the days passed, the weather worsened. The situation became dire for Pike and his men. Trekking through the cold without adequate supplies put the men at risk of starvation and frostbite. The rough journey left them exhausted, and several fell ill. Unable to continue walking due to the pain in their feet, two men were left behind in the mountains. Pike promised the men he would come back for them, but they were still afraid they were being abandoned.

A week later, Pike stopped the team's advance. He believed he had completed a key mission objective—

finding the Red River. He decided to build a stockade to protect and shelter him and his men until the spring thaw arrived and they could begin the journey home.

However, Pike had not found the Red River. Instead, the lost explorers had reached the Rio Conejos, a tributary of the Rio Grande. But Pike and his team were not supposed to be anywhere near the Rio Conejos. They had crossed out of the United States and into Spanish territory, where explorers were strictly forbidden to go.

FORT ON THE RIO CONEJOS

On the west bank of the Rio Conejos, Pike and his men built a fort that was approximately 36 feet (11 m) long on each side. They used heavy cottonwood logs, each about two feet (0.6 m) in diameter to build the walls. Then they piled smaller logs on top of those, making

Unsteady Horses

During Pike's journey, the harsh winter weather affected the animals just as much as it did the men. Crossing frozen rivers proved incredibly difficult for the horses, because their hooves had no traction on the ice. Several horses slipped and fell and were injured. When it became too difficult to move the horses across the frozen water, Pike had his team lead them up over the snow-covered hills. This did not make any difference. The horses stumbled on rocks and slid down the mountainsides. Soon, none of the animals were strong enough to carry a load. The men had to build sleds to carry their supplies.

Headwaters of the Rio Grande

the walls 12 feet (3.7 m) high. They built bastions, or lookout towers, at two of the fort's corners. For extra protection, they positioned the back of the fort against the river, which was too deep and wide to be crossed at that spot.

Around the outside walls of the fort, the men dug a narrow ditch. Then they planted long, thin, sharpened sticks in the walls. The pointed tips of the sticks rose above the walls to prevent anyone from scaling over the fort. They also carved small holes in the wood, out of which they could fire their guns if necessary.

Outside, the men dug a four-foot-wide (1.2 m) moat and filled it with water. They used the dirt they dug up from making the moat to strengthen the outer base of the fort. The thick, extra layer of mud would help stop any bullets from penetrating the walls.

For an entrance, the men cut a small hole at the bottom of one wall. Then they stretched a wooden plank across the ditch. To enter the fort, the men had to lie on their stomachs and crawl along the plank.

Pike kept a sentry posted outside the fort at

In Good Company

Zebulon Montgomery Pike, an often-forgotten explorer, was only one of many who ventured west. Others also journeyed westward:

- Captains Meriwether Lewis and William Clark explored waterways leading to the Pacific (1804–1806).
- Sacagawea, a Shoshone woman, served as an interpreter and guide for the Lewis and Clark expedition.
- John Colter traveled with Lewis and Clark, but left them to explore Yellowstone on his own (1804–1808).
- William Sublette located the Yellowstone geysers (1826).
- Jedediah Smith explored routes between the Great Salt Lake and California (1826).
- Benjamin Bonneville explored Wyoming Territory (1832).
- John C. Frémont explored the Pacific Northwest (1842–1844).
- Christopher "Kit" Carson guided groups of travelers through the Northwest, California, and New Mexico (1842–1846).

all times to watch for any intruders. Building the fort no doubt saved the explorers' lives. It provided them shelter from the elements and allowed them to rest in relative safety. But they were not yet out of harm's way.

The group of explorers included a doctor, which was very rare under the circumstances. Frostbite had set into several of the men's toes and feet. For some, the frostbite was so severe that they needed to have their toes amputated.

The weather and its effects were not the only problems for Pike's team. Although Pike had proven to be very resistant to the cold, he had pushed his men hard, and they grew unhappy with his leadership methods. One of the men tried to speak to Pike about the concerns of the team, but Pike became angry when he heard the complaints. He refused to listen to any protests.

Frostbite

Frostbite can occur when body tissue is exposed to temperatures below freezing. Fingers, toes, hands, feet, noses, ears, and chins are susceptible to frostbite because they are small and freeze quickly.

If a body part is exposed long enough, it freezes, and circulation is cut off to the affected part. Without blood flowing through it, the tissue will die. With surface frostbite, the skin turns numb and may peel as the tissue is thawed.

Deeper frostbite can produce blood- or fluid-filled blisters. As a frozen body part is thawed, the tissue releases a poison into the blood. This can cause simple irritation or severe heart trouble.

When the tissue is frozen for so long that it dies, frostbite can lead to gangrene. The body part must be amputated, or removed from the body, before the gangrene spreads to more tissue.

LOST ON PURPOSE?

The men's frustrations and concerns did not subside. Had they come the wrong way? Why had Pike led them through such bad weather? Why had they waited so long to stop and build a fort? Part of their mission was to explore the Red River, but the mission did not have to be completed during the winter months. There did not seem to be any good explanations.

Pike was also concerned, and he was baffled by the western terrain. He carried a compass and other instruments to help him with navigation and mapping. He also had two maps with him that were drawn by other travelers. However, these maps were not very detailed in their descriptions of the landscape over which Pike and his men were traveling. Pike very well could have gotten lost due to the inaccuracies of the maps. But perhaps he went out of his way on purpose and intentionally led his team into Spanish territory. This might have been his plan all along—to get close enough to spy on the Spanish settlers.

If Pike had a reason for leading his men into Spanish territory, he was taking a very big risk. The governments of Spain and the United States had a fragile relationship. A band of U.S. explorers discovered wandering in Spanish territory could meet disastrous consequences.

FINALLY FOUND

Indeed, the Spanish suspected that something was not right. While Pike and his men were busy building their fort and warming their frozen limbs, a force of more than 100 Spanish dragoons rode through the countryside, searching for the lost explorers. The Spanish government had learned of Pike's journey, and it feared that his team would enter their land. The Spanish planned to stop him.

The Spanish riders reached Rio Conejos on February 26, 1807, and surrounded Pike's tiny fort. There was no way the frostbitten, sickly team of less than a dozen men could battle such an impressive force. Pike's only hope was to negotiate an agreement

Dragoons

Dragoons are specially trained soldiers who ride into battle on horseback. This type of military unit was used widely throughout Europe for centuries. British, French, Spanish, German, Danish, Russian, and other armies all used dragoons.

Dragoons were used by the United States as well. During the Revolutionary War, General George Washington organized several dragoon regiments within the colonies. The new United States formed its first dragoon unit in 1792 and established more in the following years. By the time the Civil War began in 1861, the dragoon units had been reorganized under the U.S. Army and officially renamed the First Regiment of Cavalry. In today's U.S. Army, a few units still bear the name cavalry, including several tank-driving squadrons.

Language Issues

Pike did not speak much Spanish, and the Spanish dragoon leaders did not speak much English. They conducted their negotiations in French, though neither side was fully fluent in that language, either. Pike carried a French dictionary and grammar book with him and consulted the texts several times while trying to negotiate with the Spanish delegation.

with the dragoon leaders before a fight ensued.

The next few days would change the course of the Pike expedition. Whether the change would make things better or worse for Pike remained a mystery. The arrival of the Spanish could mean capture or even death for Pike and his men. Would Pike's team ever make it back home? ﹏

*Pike and his men had been lost in the snowy mountains
until the Spanish arrived.*

President Thomas Jefferson

MIND-SET OF
EXPLORATION

In the early 1800s, the United States was still a young nation. The country occupied less than half of the area it covers today. Only seventeen states and two territories made up the union. Settlers gradually began moving west toward the wide-open spaces that were still mostly uncharted and unknown.

The nation's third president, Thomas Jefferson, knew that it was important to gather as much information as possible about the land west of the Mississippi River. In order to do that, he needed the help of explorers.

The Louisiana Purchase

In 1803, President Jefferson completed the Louisiana Purchase, in which France sold an enormous plot of land west of the Mississippi River to the United States. The United States did not know exactly what it was buying, and France did not know how much land it was selling. The land acquired in the deal included areas that are now the present-day states of Louisiana, Oklahoma, Arkansas, Missouri,

**President
Thomas Jefferson**

By the time Jefferson became president in 1801, he was already an experienced statesman. He served in the Virginia House of Burgesses and the Continental Congress. He was known for being quiet, but his written words were eloquent and well respected. Perhaps his most famous words are those of the Declaration of Independence, which he drafted in 1776. After the American Revolution, he served as minister to France, secretary of state for President George Washington, and vice president to President John Adams.

After his second term in office, Jefferson retired to Monticello, his estate in Virginia. He helped found the University of Virginia in his later years. Jefferson died on July 4, 1826.

Map of the Louisiana Purchase

Kansas, Nebraska, Iowa, South Dakota, Minnesota, Montana, Wyoming, Colorado, New Mexico, and Texas.

The total area of the Louisiana Purchase covered 827,987 square miles (2,144,476.5 sq km). This huge expanse of land doubled the size of the United States.

The new land meant many new opportunities for the young nation. But first, the region needed to be explored, mapped, and eventually settled. This was both an exciting and unpredictable process.

The Louisiana Purchase also created challenges for the country. The boundaries of the new land bordered Spanish-ruled Mexico. Suddenly, diplomatic relations with Spain became much more complicated. The United States would also confront more groups of Native Americans, whose homelands had just been acquired by the country.

WESTWARD EXPANSION

Jefferson encouraged exploration of the new western region. He believed that there had to be a way to transport goods, by river, across the North American continent from the

An Unexpected Purchase

President Jefferson sent Secretary of State James Monroe to France to negotiate the purchase of a small piece of land. Jefferson authorized Monroe to offer $10 million for the port city of New Orleans. Much to Monroe's shock, Napoleon offered the United States a vastly larger piece of land for just $5 million more. Monroe was not authorized to purchase so much land or to spend that much money, but he decided on the spot that the offer was too good to pass up. He was certain that Jefferson would approve.

Jefferson was torn when Monroe told him of the deal. Although more land meant more opportunity for the United States, the Constitution did not permit the purchase of new land. New laws would have to be created to make the purchase legal. To work around this, the purchase was set up as a treaty with France. Treaties were allowed under the Constitution. The treaty was drafted in France on April 30, 1803, and signed on May 2. It was ratified by the Congress in October 1803. The United States took possession of the land that December.

Lewis and Clark Expedition

Meriwether Lewis and William Clark departed from St. Louis on May 14, 1804. They led a party of 22 men in search of the Northwest Passage.

Lewis and Clark discovered that there was no all-water route to the Pacific Ocean. Nonetheless, they established relationships with Native American tribes, explored and mapped a large portion of the new territory, and strengthened the nation's claim to a new piece of land—the Oregon Territory.

Atlantic Ocean to the Pacific. A few weeks after completing the purchase, Jefferson asked Congress to grant him $2,500 for an expedition. He hoped the expedition would lead to the discovery of the Northwest Passage, an undiscovered water route running across the county. He commissioned Captain Meriwether Lewis to lead the expedition— afterward known as the Corps of Discovery—to find the waterway that connected the Missouri River to the Pacific Ocean. Lewis chose William Clark, a captain in the U.S. Army, to lead the expedition with him.

Lewis was Jefferson's personal secretary and a trusted associate. Jefferson made sure Lewis received specialized training in navigation and exploration. Lewis also studied botany and zoology so that he could identify and describe the plants and animals he discovered during his journey.

Meriwether Lewis, left, and William Clark

Lewis spent approximately one year preparing for his expedition and gathering the team of men who would travel with him during the expedition that would take them 3,700 (5954.6 km) miles from the Mississippi River to the Pacific Ocean.

Lewis and Clark departed from St. Louis in May 1804, approximately two years before Zebulon Montgomery Pike would venture west to embark on a very different kind of exploration.

Native Americans

Jefferson knew that the Louisiana Purchase would lead to the displacement of Native Americans from their land. The United States had already established the practice of pushing Native American tribes westward to make room for white settlers. Most tribes were angry over this intrusion, and they were willing to fight for their land.

The United States tried to use diplomacy when dealing with the Native Americans. This was one of the key objectives of western exploration. The country sent people to talk with tribal leaders in an effort to convince them to move west quietly

A Peaceful Future

President Jefferson knew that in order for the nation to expand, many Native Americans would have to be moved from their land. Though he was not bothered by this idea, he knew that it should be kept quiet to avoid conflict with the tribes. In a letter to one governor, Jefferson wrote:

"[We must] live in perpetual peace with the Indians . . . for their interests and their tranquility it is best they should see only the present age of their history."[1]

and peacefully, out of the way of the settlers. In some cases, the government offered to purchase their land. Sometimes the diplomatic efforts succeeded, and the tribes moved without putting up a struggle. Often, though, they did not. The Native American tribes and settlers engaged in many battles along the western frontier. The tribes lost the bulk of these conflicts and were driven from their land.

RELATIONS WITH SPAIN

Following the Louisiana Purchase, the United States' relationship with Spain became tense. Spain did not feel that France had a legal right to sell the territory. Further, the Louisiana Purchase agreement was not specific about the exact southwestern boundary of the land.

The United States and Spain had a fundamental disagreement over the territorial boundaries of the Louisiana Purchase. Spain believed it included the piece of land that includes the present-day states of Louisiana and Arkansas. The United States believed it included all of the drainages of the Missouri River, including the Arkansas River in the Southwest and the Rio Grande and Red River in the South.

If an agreement was not reached soon, there could be disastrous consequences. It was eventually decided that the border would be drawn between the Rio Grande and the Red River. Leaders of both countries agreed to mark the Sabine River as the border. Despite this agreement, however, the matter was never completely settled. In 1805, Spanish soldiers crossed the Sabine River into U.S. territory. U.S. soldiers were waiting near the Red River, where they had built a fort. It seemed that a war would soon break out.

The tension between Spain and the United States created turmoil in the West. People did not know what was going to happen. General James Wilkinson, governor of the Louisiana Purchase territory, saw this uncertainty as an opportunity.

THE WILKINSON-BURR PLOT

While Jefferson put his energy toward exploring and settling Louisiana, Wilkinson and another political leader—Vice President Aaron Burr—had other plans for the western territory. Burr had desperately wanted to be president. His loss to Jefferson in the 1800 election left him bitter. If Burr could not be president of the United States, he was determined to form a nation of his own, and he found an ally in Wilkinson.

Wilkinson and Burr met secretly in June 1805. They spent several days together at Fort Massac, located on the Ohio River. Both men had grand ideas about the future of the West. They were hungry for power, and they were willing to do some wrong in order to get it.

Wilkinson and Burr discussed creating a private army, one whose soldiers did not have to answer to the U.S. government. They planned to use this force to invade Mexico and take it away from the Spanish. Once Mexico was free, many trade opportunities would become available. Wilkinson and Burr planned to profit from those opportunities.

Wanting to create a new nation they could control, Wilkinson and Burr also plotted to separate the

Duel to the Death

Thomas Jefferson and Aaron Burr were two among several presidential candidates in 1800. The election ended as a tie between them. Congress voted to decide which man would be president and which man would be vice president.

Alexander Hamilton, a prominent member of the Congress, spoke out against Burr. Jefferson ended up winning the vote.

Angry over the election outcome, Burr challenged Hamilton to a duel. On July 11, 1804, the pair faced each other with loaded pistols. Burr shot Hamilton in the duel. Hamilton died the next day.

Louisiana Purchase territory from the nation. They planned to encourage some of the states, including Tennessee and Kentucky, to separate from the Union and join their new republic. Zebulon Montgomery Pike would soon play a vital role in this secret plot. ⁓

Vice President Aaron Burr

Zebulon Montgomery Pike

A CHALLENGING LIFE

"Nothing that Zebulon Montgomery Pike ever tried to do was easy, and most of his luck was bad," someone once wrote.[1] Pike indeed faced many problems during his expeditions. His life before his explorations was filled with challenges, too. Pike had to make many difficult decisions, each with its own consequences. Scholars who study Pike's life debate whether the choices he made were good, and why he did the things he did.

Young Zeb

Zebulon Montgomery Pike was born on January 5, 1779, in Lamberton, New Jersey, near the present-day city of Trenton. Zeb, as he was called as a child, was the oldest of his living siblings. His parents were Isabella and Zebulon Pike. Young Zeb was named after his father. Isabella gave birth to eight children, but four of them died as babies. Zeb's younger brothers and sister, James, George, and Maria, all struggled with tuberculosis (then called consumption), a lung disease. They were unhealthy all their lives. Zeb, however, was an unusually strong, healthy boy. He would grow into a man who could withstand difficult physical challenges.

When Zeb was just two years old, the family moved from New Jersey to Pennsylvania. They tried farming in several different locations, but it was difficult to make a living. They moved farther and farther west, like many other settlers were doing at the time. Zeb's father had been a soldier in the

American Revolution, which ended in 1783. When farming became too difficult, he put his military skill to use again by joining the Pennsylvania militia. He was well paid for the work, which involved defending the new settlers from attacks by the Native American tribes, whose land was being taken for the white settlers.

When Zeb was 14 years old, his father gained a command post at Fort Washington, which was located on the Ohio River near the present-day city of Cincinnati, Ohio. Young Zeb spent his teen years there and became quite

Tuberculosis

Tuberculosis is a disease caused by bacteria that normally affects the lungs. A person's kidneys, spine, brain, and other organs can also be affected. Common tuberculosis symptoms include coughing, fatigue, fever, chest pains, severe cough, and extreme weight loss.

Tuberculosis bacteria spread through the air. When a person who has the disease coughs or sneezes, other people who breathe in the same air may become ill. However, not everyone who breathes tuberculosis bacteria gets sick. When bacteria appear in the body, the immune system fights the disease. People with weaker immune systems, such as young children, the elderly, or people who are already ill, are at greater risk for contracting tuberculosis.

Tuberculosis used to be called consumption, because it consumed the bodies of the people it infected and often resulted in death. For many years, it was one of the most common illnesses in the United States and other parts of the world.

In the 1940s, scientists created medicines that could treat tuberculosis, though there is still no cure. People still become infected with tuberculosis today, but new treatments are being developed that keep the disease under control.

intrigued by the soldiers and the happenings at the fort.

Hero Worship

Pike enjoyed watching the inner workings of the army at the fort. Following in his father's footsteps, Pike became a cadet in the army at 15. His first assignment was sending supplies to the troops stationed in the area. Pike particularly admired General James Wilkinson, an officer based at Fort Washington. More than anything, Pike wanted to be noticed by the general.

Pike was a stubborn and willful young man, and these traits stayed with him into adulthood. Once he set his sights on something, he worked tirelessly to make it happen. His goal was to become a successful soldier and distinguish himself from other young men his age.

While other young men went out drinking, fighting, and gambling,

It Runs in the Family

Pike enlisted in the army when he was 15 years old. Years later, Pike's younger brother, George, enlisted in the army at the same age. Pike was extremely proud of his brother and wrote him letters encouraging him to be brave and fight hard.

Pike's father held a compound post at Fort Washington.

Pike stayed in and studied. He had little formal
schooling, but he took it upon himself to study
hard. He focused on mathematics and French in
particular, subjects he believed would help him
become an effective leader. He was also a good
athlete, excelled at shooting, and loved the outdoors.

In 1796, Wilkinson became a senior officer of
the U.S. Army. Eventually, Wilkinson noticed Pike's

performance. In 1799, Wilkinson promoted Pike twice within the span of a few months, first making him second lieutenant and later, lieutenant.

Pike Falls in Love

In his early twenties, Pike fell in love with his cousin, Clarissa Brown. She was an educated and studious girl, and they had much in common. Clarissa's father, Captain James Brown, did not think Pike was good enough for his daughter. He refused to give Pike her hand in marriage, but Pike and Clarissa's love would not be denied. In 1801, the young couple eloped.

Pike and Clarissa's marriage created a divide between their families. Though Pike and Clarissa remained happily married, the families were never able to mend their differences. Pike's decision to marry Clarissa without her father's approval was an example of young Pike's stubbornness and determination.

Pike's Hero Assigns a Mission

In 1803, Pike and Clarissa were stationed at Fort Kaskaskia on the Mississippi River, south of St. Louis. Pike became the commander of the fort,

Wilkinson's Schemes

Young Pike probably had no way of knowing how devious his hero, General Wilkinson, was. In 1777, Wilkinson had been involved in a conspiracy, led by General Thomas Conway, to replace George Washington as leader of the Revolutionary Army. When the plot failed, Wilkinson turned informant against Conway.

Ten years later, Wilkinson struck a deal with the Spanish to become a double agent. He was paid $2,000 a year to pass secret information about U.S. Army activities. Wilkinson's experience with treason would eventually make him a perfect partner for Aaron Burr, who also had plans to undermine the U.S. Army.

a good post for someone so young. Soon after they arrived, Captain Meriwether Lewis passed through the fort to gather a team of soldiers to accompany him on his expedition. Some of Pike's own men became recruits of Lewis's, and they left with him when he departed for his westward voyage.

Wilkinson had plans for Pike. In 1805, Wilkinson was made governor of Upper Louisiana (the portion of the Louisiana Purchase north of the boundaries of present-day Louisiana). This position gave Wilkinson greater power, which he used to his every advantage. Wilkinson summoned Pike to St. Louis, where a special assignment awaited him.

General James Wilkinson

Pike exploring the land at the headwaters of the Mississippi River

THE FIRST EXPEDITION

General Wilkinson sent Pike north to explore the headwaters of the Mississippi River to find its true source, which would mark the northernmost border of the Louisiana Purchase. This assignment began in secret. Unlike the explorations of Lewis and Clark, which President

Jefferson had encouraged, Pike's journey to the headwaters of the Mississippi River began before Wilkinson informed Jefferson. This was one of many actions Wilkinson took without getting the president's approval.

Wilkinson often acted in his own interest, so the real purpose behind Pike's mission may not have been what it seemed. The area Pike was to travel through was fairly well-known, but Wilkinson wanted Pike to learn more about the French and British fur traders who had settled in the area that is the present-day state of Minnesota. Wilkinson was planning to make a deal with some of the French settlers, in hopes of making money from the fur trade.

The journey seemed easy and straightforward, but there were complications. Pike's assignment was to follow the river and study the fur traders, but Wilkinson also wanted him to communicate with the Native Americans. Some of the tribes Pike met were hostile about the invasion of European and U.S. settlers into their territory, making it difficult for Pike to establish friendly relationships with them. Wilkinson also asked Pike to purchase land on which to build new forts and trading posts.

THE JOURNEY BEGINS

Pike and his team of 20 men set out on August 9, 1805. They carried four months' worth of supplies in a keelboat. They brought tents, clothing, and gunpowder, as well as basic food supplies, including salt, flour, and cornmeal. They also packed special stocks of items such as whiskey, tobacco, hunting knives, and cloth, which they used to trade with the Native Americans. They did not have a doctor or an interpreter with them, nor did they have sufficient navigation equipment.

The Mississippi River flows south, but Pike and his men had to travel north to reach its headwaters. They had to row against the river's current, which was not easy. Physical obstacles such as submerged logs and sandbars often got in their way. At one point, a large floating log tore a hole in the side of the keelboat, causing water to flow in. The men hauled the boat out of the river, repaired the hole with fresh wood, and dried their wet

Feast or Famine

Pike and his men set out with some basic food supplies in their boat— salt, flour, and cornmeal. But it was impossible to bring along enough food to last the entire journey. The team needed protein to maintain their strength, so they fished and hunted along the way. Some of the small animals they hunted and ate included ducks, geese, rabbits, and raccoons. They also ate large game, such as deer and bison. Each man could eat approximately 7 to 8 pounds (3.1 to 3.6 kg) of meat per day.

belongings before they continued. On days when such setbacks occurred, the explorers did not make much progress.

The keelboat Pike and his men traveled in was made of wood. It was 70 feet (21.3 m) long. The boat had one large sail made of canvas, and when the men were fortunate enough to catch a good wind, it helped carry them across the water quickly. If there was no wind, the men rowed with oars or used long poles to move the boat forward. Sometimes they would take turns walking along the river bank while towing the boat with ropes. This was slow, difficult work.

Mississippi River

The Mississippi River is a constantly changing body of water. Its length, width, depth, and volume change over time, so it is impossible to determine its exact size and shape. The measurements change slightly each day. Scientists study the Mississippi closely and observe its effects on the physical world and the people around it. More than 50 cities rely on the Mississippi for their water supply.

The Mississippi is approximately 2,300 miles (3,701 km) long. At Lake Itasca, its narrowest point, the river is approximately 20 to 30 feet (6.1 to 9.1 m) wide. At Lake Onalaska in Wisconsin, the river's widest point measures approximately four miles (6.4 km) across. The river is shallowest at its headwaters—only about 3 feet (.9 m) deep—but it is more than 200 feet (61 m) deep at Algers Point in New Orleans, where it flows into the Gulf of Mexico.

The river is also slowest at its Lake Itasca headwaters, where it moves approximately 1.2 miles (1.9 km) an hour, the rate of a slow walk. In New Orleans, the river flows three times faster. The basin is deeper and wider as well, so more water moves through it at once.

NATIVE HELP

On August 20, 1805, Pike and his team reached the present-day state of Iowa. They came to a particularly rough section of the Mississippi River and struggled to paddle through the rapids. A group of Sauk Indians helped them. The next day, Pike met with the Sauk chief and gave him knives, tobacco, and whiskey.

Pike and his team then continued up the river. When the men reached Prairie du Chien a few weeks later, Pike's crew abandoned the keelboat and adopted two barges. Each had a large cannon at the front. Pike most likely knew that the Native Americans he and his men would soon encounter would disapprove of these warships. Still, Pike and his men headed up the river in the new boats.

LAND DEAL

On September 23, 1805, they reached the area where the cities of Minneapolis and St. Paul would later be established. Pike found a plot of land that he thought would be suitable for building a fort. He negotiated with the Sioux leaders to purchase it and promised them $200,000 for 155,000 acres (62,726 ha).

Bluffs overlooking the Mississippi River near Prairie du Chien

Pike ascended the Falls of St. Anthony, another tricky section of river, just as the winter weather set in. The water grew frigid, and Pike's men began to fall ill. Pike wanted to keep going, but he realized his men would not last much longer if they continued.

WINTER CAMP

Pike and his men traveled from the Falls of St. Anthony to an area near the present-day city of Little Falls, Minnesota. They stopped and built a small stockade. The men were relieved to be resting in a shelter out of the cold winter elements. Still, Pike wanted to continue moving north, despite the

The Fur Trade

When Europeans first arrived in North America in the 1500s, they traded goods with the Native Americans. This included exchanging knives or tools for animal furs. Beaver, mink, otter, and fox furs became popular with the French and British, and the trade expanded.

Formal fur trading businesses developed, such as the Hudson Bay Company, which was established in the present-day country of Canada. British and French traders fought over territory. These disagreements contributed to the outbreak of the French and Indian War in 1754.

The fur trade slowed during the 1800s as the demand for furs decreased. Also, many of the animals had grown scarce from centuries of trapping activity.

weather. But the river was no longer a viable travel option—the water was simply too cold, and in some places, it was frozen. Realizing that traveling by boat was no longer feasible, Pike decided to use sleds. He took half of his men with him, leaving the others to ride out the winter at the stockade.

Moving north through deep snows and below-zero temperatures, Pike and his men risked severe illness and frostbite to complete their mission. At several points along the way, British fur trappers and traders offered them shelter. Despite the warm hospitality Pike and his men received from the trappers, Pike informed the British that they were no longer welcome in U.S. territory. Pike was helping Wilkinson execute his plan—move out the British trappers and traders to make room for the American trappers. That would bring the fur trade profits back to St. Louis.

LEECH LAKE

Pike arrived at the Leech Lake trading post on February 1, 1806. The site was occupied by a British fur trader named Hugh McGillis, who was flying the flag of his nation. Seeing the British flag flying over U.S. territory deeply offended Pike. He was very patriotic, and as a representative of a young nation seeking respect and control of its own territory, he asked McGillis to take it down. When McGillis refused to lower the British colors, Pike ordered his men to shoot the flag off its pole.

Pike mistakenly believed he had found the source of the Mississippi River at Leech Lake. At a fork in the river, he had followed the left branch instead of the right, which brought him to Leech Lake. Had he followed the right branch, he would have discovered Lake Itasca, the river's true source, which was approximately 20 miles (32.2 km) farther northwest.

What's in a Name?

Henry Schoolcraft was an American explorer, geographer, geologist, and ethnologist. He realized that Pike was wrong in claiming that Leech Lake was the true source of the Mississippi River when he discovered its true source in 1832. Schoolcraft named the body of water Lake Itasca. He took the letters *I, T, A, S, C,* and *A* from the Latin words *veritas* and *caput,* which mean "truth" and "head," respectively.

**Sergeant Kennerman's
Yard Sale**

When Pike returned from Leech Lake to the stockade at the present-day city of Little Falls, Minnesota, he discovered an unpleasant surprise. Or perhaps it was what he did not discover that bothered him. One of the men he had left behind, Sergeant Kennerman, had sold all of the items out of Pike's personal trunk and given away all of the team's stores of food and meat. Pike immediately demoted the sergeant to a private.

HEADING HOME

Pike believed his mission to be complete and turned his team southward, back toward the stockade to regroup with the rest of the team. He was prepared to report Leech Lake as the Mississippi's source. He was also going to inform Wilkinson that he had ordered all British fur traders to leave the area (though they never followed his instructions). Although Pike had not been able to convince any Native American tribal leaders to accompany him back to St. Louis, he considered his work complete. He had communicated with tribal leaders in their own lands and had acquired a plot of land on which to build a U.S. fort.

It was spring 1806 when Pike and his men returned to St. Louis. Pike was quite ready for a rest. But as it turned out, he would not be home for very long. —

Trappers finding a beaver in a leghold trap

Zebulon Montgomery Pike

THE SECOND EXPEDITION

ike had only been back in St. Louis for a few weeks when General Wilkinson presented him with another mission. The general's plotting with Aaron Burr had intensified. Although the ultimate objective of their conspiracy is not clear, it is believed that they planned to take over the western United States and create a separate nation. To succeed, their plan required a journey west. Wilkinson decided to send his most loyal soldier— Pike.

Pike still deeply admired the general. He was thrilled to be chosen to lead a second, more important expedition. He would do everything he could to make the general proud.

PIKE'S NEW ASSIGNMENT

Pike's assignment had three main objectives. First, he had to escort a group of Osage Indians from St. Louis back to their home in the area of the present-day state of Missouri. Second, he was to talk to leaders of several Native American tribes. Part of this task involved negotiating peace between the warring Kansas and Pawnee tribes. The other part was to seek out and establish communication with the Comanche tribe. Finally, Pike was ordered to explore the headwaters of the Arkansas and Red rivers.

There was likely a fourth, secret element to the expedition. If possible, Pike was to reach New Spain and gather information about its people, settlements, and military forces. This involved him entering, without permission, an area ruled by Spain. How any information Pike gained from spying on the Spanish settlers would help Wilkinson's plot to take over the West is unclear. However, it is known that Wilkinson often traded U.S. secrets to the Spanish government in exchange for money. Perhaps he wanted to add to the already tense relationship between Spain and the United States.

It is difficult to ascertain why Wilkinson trusted Pike with this important mission. Perhaps Pike's loyalty and admiration for Wilkinson ensured

---

The Prairie Dog

Pike made notes of the many species of wildlife he encountered during his missions. He mentioned bison, buffalo, elk, and deer, all of which his men hunted for food. He also noted wolves, badgers, snakes, tortoises, horned toads, and chameleons living in the grasses.

Among his favorites were prairie dogs, though Pike called them prairie squirrels. He marveled at the animals' cleverness at building homes in elevated spots where they had access to drinking water, but would not be flooded out of their holes. He wrote more:

> They are of a dark brown color, except their bellies, which are white . . . their teeth head, nails, and body are the perfect squirrel, except that they are generally fatter than that animal. Their villages sometimes extend over two and three miles square, in which there must be innumerable hosts of them, as there is generally a burrow every ten steps in which there are two or more, and you see new ones partly excavated on all the borders of the town.[1]

Pike's account of these animal societies was one of the first to be published.

his position as the right man for the job. Wilkinson knew he could trust Pike to do what he asked, whether or not those actions were in the nation's best interest.

Pike was not as educated, experienced, and prepared as he needed to be when he set out west on July 15, 1806. Pike's journey would be challenging, and he faced some nearly impossible tasks. Possible failure did not stop Pike, however, and he took dangerous risks in an effort to prove his worth.

MAN ON A MISSION

"We sailed from the landing at Belle Fontaine, about 3 o'clock P.M. in two boats," Pike wrote in his journal on July 15, 1806.[2] He left St. Louis that day with 23 men in his party of explorers. General Wilkinson's son, Lieutenant James Wilkinson, was among them, as was a physician named John Robinson. A close associate of Wilkinson, the doctor had been given special orders to follow during the trip. Soldiers made up the rest of Pike's team. Also traveling with them were 51 Native Americans from the Osage and Pawnee tribes. Some were tribal leaders who had traveled to Washington to meet with President Jefferson. The others had been captured

The Osage

Centuries before European settlers set foot on the continent, the Osage tribe lived in the central plains of North America. Their territory once covered the plains west of the Mississippi River, south of the Missouri River, and north of the Arkansas River.

French fur traders first made contact with the Osage in the 1670s. From that point on, the Osage tribe was subject to intense pressure to move off its land and give it up to the incoming Europeans. In 1825, as settlers poured into the newly formed state of Missouri, the Osage were pushed into a small swath of land in Kansas. Almost 50 years later in 1872, the Osage Reservation was established in Oklahoma.

by a Potawatomi tribe and were later freed by a ransom paid by the United States.

Pike's team was to escort the Osage and Pawnee to their homes. First, they followed the Missouri and Osage rivers to the Osage homeland in the present-day state of Missouri. The tribe was pleased at the homecoming of its lost members, and the Osage looked kindly on their American visitors.

HUNTED

Pike and his men continued on to a Pawnee village, located on the border of the present-day states of Kansas and Nebraska. They arrived in late September 1806. The Pawnee chief, White Wolf, was not surprised to see them. He informed Pike that a huge party of Spanish soldiers had recently ridden into the area, searching for a band of U.S. explorers. Even though the Spanish troops were actually searching for Lewis and Clark—based on information that had been provided to them by General Wilkinson—Pike and his team were in danger.

Pike spent time negotiating with the Pawnee chief, with little success. White Wolf refused to sell Pike enough horses to supply his team, provide him with an interpreter, or tell him in which direction the Spanish force had ridden. White Wolf did his best to discourage Pike from continuing his mission. From the Pawnees' point of view, the fewer white people who crossed their land, the better.

Unable to secure much help from the Pawnee tribe, Pike and his team set out to find the rivers they were supposed to explore. They searched for and found the trail left by the Spanish riders, heading south toward the Arkansas River.

Bigger Problems

When Pike asked White Wolf to point him in the direction the Spanish had traveled, the Pawnee chief laughed. He thought it was foolish of Pike to pursue the large force of Spanish troops. White Wolf told Pike that if he needed a guide to help him find the trail of the Spanish, he should ask the village idiot to show him the way. The Spanish force consisted of some 600 men and 2,500 horses. Walking along the plains, the animals left a trampled grass trail as wide as a football field wherever they went. White Wolf's point was that if Pike's men could not find such a trail on their own, they had much bigger problems. Pike's men did eventually find the massive trail.

Pike's Party

- Lieutenant James Wilkinson
- Doctor John Robinson
- Sergeant Joseph Ballenger
- Sergeant William Meek
- Corporal Jeremiah R. Jackson
- Private John Boley
- Private Samuel Bradley
- Private John Brown
- Private Jacob Carter
- Private Thomas Dougherty
- Private William Gordon
- Private Solomon Huddleston
- Private Henry Kennerman
- Private Theodore Miller
- Private Hugh Menaugh
- Private John Mountjoy
- Private Alexander Roy
- Private Patrick Smith
- Private John Sparks
- Private Freegift Stout
- Private John Wilson
- Baroney Vasquez, interpreter

THE PARTY SPLITS

In mid-October 1806, Pike's party reached the Arkansas River. At that point, the group split up to complete two separate missions. Pike would continue searching for the headwaters, while Lieutenant Wilkinson would lead a small group back to St. Louis. This split had been planned from the beginning. Young Wilkinson was to explore the lower parts of the Arkansas River and provide a report to his father about the success of the first half of the journey.

The men built a cottonwood canoe and another boat made of sticks and buffalo hides. Departing on October 28, 1806, Lieutenant Wilkinson, five other soldiers, and two Osage rowed these crafts east along the Arkansas River. Wintry weather set in, and the river began to freeze over. Wilkinson worried that ice in the river would slow his

Pike's party split into two groups when it reached the Arkansas River.

small group's progress and that they might not have enough supplies to make it home.

The next day, Pike's party came to the path left by the Spanish riders. They followed the path to the point where it turned toward Santa Fe. Plodding into the cold, Pike and his men continued following the Arkansas River. The next phase of their journey would be the most trying, by far. ⌒

*Three people representing different Native American tribes—
the Osage, the Iroquois, and the Pawnee*

Aerial view of the Rocky Mountains

THE WINTER CAMPAIGN

*P*ike and the rest of the team proceeded westward. Soon, the few horses they had acquired from the Pawnee began to give out. The animals were starving after weeks of eating only tree bark and dead leaves, and they were growing weak.

The men, however, ate well. They encountered vast herds of buffalo on the plains. Pike and his men would kill numerous bison in a single day, providing the men with hundreds of pounds of meat.

On November 15, 1806, Pike and his men caught sight of the Rocky Mountains in the distance. Ten days later, Pike stopped the team's advance. They quickly built a shelter, a three-sided wood structure approximately five feet (1.5 m) tall. Leaving most of the men at the new camp, Pike set off to climb the tallest of the nearby mountains.

To Climb the Grand Peak

Pike took three men with him to climb the mountain—Doctor Robinson, Private Brown, and Private Miller. Pike wanted to climb the mountain so he could survey the landscape from the top, looking for clues as to which directions the

Each Pair for Itself

When they were deep in the mountains, instead of traveling as a group, Pike broke the team into pairs. They marched two by two through the snow. The men in front would hunt and leave the animal carcasses behind for the others.

The Grand Peak

At first sight, Pike described the mountain as "a small blue cloud." When he left his men at camp, he thought it would take him only a few days to reach the base of the mountain. The Grand Peak, as he called it, turned out to be much farther away—more than 150 miles (241 km)—across another smaller mountain range.

Pike never made it to the mountain that now bears his name. The foothill he climbed to get a better look at the Grand Peak may have been Mount Rosa, near the present-day city of Colorado Springs, Colorado.

rivers flowed. They hiked across the plains to where they thought the foot of the mountain began and set up camp for the night. In the morning, they realized they had to cross several more hills before they would reach the mountain's base. They climbed these hills and camped for another night. The next morning, they left their supplies at the foot of the mountain and headed up, believing it would be only a day's journey to the mountain's summit. They were quite wrong. Pike and his men climbed too far that day to make it back down before dark fell. They were forced to spend the night huddled together in a cave in the mountainside, without blankets, food, or water.

The next day, they continued up the mountain. They reached the top, only to realize they had not climbed the highest peak, but a mere foothill. Pike theorized that it would take at least another day to reach the real mountain, let alone to climb it. It was too cold to continue. Their clothes were not warm, and they had left their supplies behind. The weary hikers turned around. When they reached the bottom, they found that their food had been eaten by animals.

Pike and the three men struggled to return to the rest of the group. They reached the rest of the team as deep winter began to set in upon the region. It was then that Pike made the decision that he and his team would continue the journey rather than wait out the harsh winter in the shelter. This misguided decision nearly resulted in the death of his entire team.

HEADWATERS OF THE ARKANSAS

Pike's team left their shelter in early December 1806. They trudged through snow drifts three feet (.9 m) deep as they began their return to the Arkansas River. They also looked for the Spanish trail, but the snows made tracking difficult. Winds swept fiercely across the bare plains, and there were few trees and no hills to provide shelter.

Within a week, Pike came to the Arkansas River. The water was freezing, and large blocks of ice drifted with the current. Still, Pike and his team had to cross it, for the next part of the mission was to head south and find the Red River.

The team waded across the icy river. The feet of two of the soldiers were so badly frostbitten that they could not go on. Eager to continue the mission, a small team of men separated from the group to follow the Arkansas River to its headwaters.

They spent a day walking along the river to a large canyon, where it became a smaller stream. They reported back to Pike that they had found the Arkansas River headwaters. They hoped this discovery would mean it was time to return home.

WANDERING

Pike had other plans. He did not lead his men home. Nor did he lead them southeast, toward the Red River and the final part of their mission. Instead, he turned northwest, searching again for the trail of the

Royal Gorge

Near Canon City, Colorado, Royal Gorge is considered the "Grand Canyon" of the Arkansas River. Royal Gorge is a popular tourist attraction today. People can walk across the bridge that spans the gorge, which is the highest suspension bridge in the world. A cable car also stretches over the canyon, and people can ride the Skycoaster for a bungee-jumping-style experience. Below the bridge, the gorge is 1,053 feet (321 m) deep. It is approximately 40 to 50 feet (12 to 15 m) wide at the bottom and more than 800 hundred feet (244 m) wide at the top.

Spanish riders. Pike's men were cold, tired, and confused by Pike's decision. They followed Pike because they had to, but they grew more discouraged with each passing day.

Pike tried to reassure his men. He insisted that he was leading them toward the Red River. After some time, they stumbled upon a small stream and began to follow it. Pike declared that it was the Red River.

However, it quickly became clear that the small stream they were following was not the Red River. In fact, this water was the true headwaters of the Arkansas River. Pike and his team soon found themselves back at their previous camp on the bank of the Arkansas. This frustrated Pike's men greatly— they had been wandering in a giant circle for an entire month. They had made no progress, and their health was getting worse.

LEFT BEHIND

Finally, Pike began leading his team south. The men were struggling, except for Pike. His strong physical health served him well, even in the worst weather. He wanted to press on.

The team's store of food staples was gone. They had no salt, flour, or dried meat remaining. They

A map, based on Pike's accounts, of the Mississippi, Missouri, Red, and Arkansas rivers

foraged for food and hunted when they were able. The team often went without food.

The men were still wearing the summer uniforms they had brought with them from St. Louis. They had no warmer clothes. They fashioned what they could out of animal hides. Some of the men tied pieces of buffalo skin around their feet to keep them from freezing. It helped, but not much.

On January 22, 1807, Pike made the difficult decision to leave some of the injured men behind. Privates John Sparks's and Thomas Dougherty's feet were frozen, and they could no longer walk. Pike left them in the snow with their guns and some ammunition. In their poor condition, though, it was unlikely that they would be able to hunt, so he gave them a few days' worth of food provisions. He also left them with some of the remaining sickly horses. Pike promised he would return for the soldiers, but he was sad to leave the men behind. "We parted, but not without tears," he wrote in his journal.[1]

Nearly Frozen

Pike and his men entered the Sangre de Cristo Mountains on January 24, 1807. Pike was soon forced to admit that he could not push his men any farther. They stopped along the banks of the Rio Conejos and built a small fort. They had officially entered Spanish territory.

True to his word, Pike sent two men back to pick up Sparks and Dougherty, the abandoned soldiers.

The Write Thing?

Pike's notes in his journal often contradict his actions. In this entry, he claims to feel deep sorrow for the men he left behind and alludes to his promise to return for them. At the time he wrote this, however, he had already failed to protect them as he vowed he would:

This evening the corporal and three of the men arrived, who had been sent back to the camp of the frozen lads. . . . the other two, Dougherty and Sparks, were unable to come.

They said that they [Sparks and Dougherty] had hailed them with tears of joy, and were in despair when they again left them, with the chance of never seeing them more. They sent on to me some of the bones taken out of their feet, and conjured me by all that was sacred, not to leave them to perish far from the civilized world.

Ah! little did they know my heart, if they could suspect me of conduct so ungenerous. No! Before they should be left, I would for months have carried the end of a litter [stretcher], in order to secure them the happiness of once more seeing their native homes and being received in the bosom of a grateful country.[2]

The team had traveled nearly 200 miles (322 km) since leaving them. Sparks and Dougherty were still alive, but they could not move. They were angry about being left behind and afraid of dying in the cold mountains. The frostbite in their legs had cut off the blood flow to their feet, resulting in gangrene. Their feet were rotting. There was no way they could walk, and Pike had not sent enough men to carry them. As a plea not to be abandoned, the soldiers cut off pieces of their toes and sent them back to Pike.

RESCUE OR CAPTURE?

On February 7, 1807, Doctor Robinson left the team and walked toward Santa Fe on his own. His special orders from General Wilkinson may have motivated him. It is not known what those orders were, specifically, but Robinson had something none of the others did—papers granting him permission to enter New Spain to collect a debt from someone in Santa Fe.

Robinson arrived in Santa Fe a few days later. He told the Spanish officials where to find Pike, and the Spanish immediately dispatched riders to apprehend the explorer.

On February 16, 1807, Pike was hunting when he encountered a Spanish dragoon and a Native American. Pike feared there would be a fight, but the riders approached him peacefully. They told him more riders were coming.

On February 26, 1807, approximately 100 Spanish dragoons rode to Pike's stockade on the Rio Conejos. Pike realized that the small fort would

not provide sufficient protection for his men.
Pike invited the Spanish leaders into the fort for
negotiations. The next few days would be tense. ⌐

Pike's group entered the snowy Sangre de Cristo Mountains in January 1807.

Santa Fe, mid-1800s

ENCOUNTERING
THE SPANISH

he arrival of the Spanish riders likely saved
Pike and his men from a cold death in the
mountains. The riders brought horses, food, and
clothing, and they shared them with Pike and his
men. More importantly, however, they knew exactly

where Pike and his team were and how to get them to where they wanted to go.

The dragoons confirmed to Pike that he and his team were nowhere near the Red River.

Captured Again

The Spanish commanders were Lieutenants Bartholomew Fernandez and Ignatio Saltelo. They entered Pike's fort to negotiate with him. When they informed Pike that he was quite a distance from the Red River, Pike responded with alarm and confusion. He immediately lowered the American flag. He tried his best not to upset the Spanish, as Wilkinson had ordered.

Fernandez and Saltelo told Pike they would give him the horses and supplies he needed to return to his own country. First, though, he would have to travel to the then-Spanish city of Santa Fe and appear before the

Denial

Doctor Robinson was at least partly responsible for the immediate rescue of Pike and his men. Still, when Pike came before Governor Alencaster, Pike repeatedly denied that Robinson had ever been a part of his team. Pike and Robinson had planned this tactic before the doctor left for Santa Fe.

governor of New Mexico. This was an order, not an offer. Pike and his men were being captured.

DEEPER INTO NEW SPAIN

Pike rode south with the Spanish dragoons. Meanwhile, the Spanish kindly sent a separate team of men to pick up Pike's frostbitten soldiers who had been left behind in the mountains.

After traveling for just a few days, the weather changed dramatically. The Spanish riders led Pike and his men out of the mountains. The air became warmer and drier as they approached the desert. It was a huge relief to Pike and his men after so many months of traveling through the unforgiving snow.

They passed through the then-Spanish town of San Juan. Along the way, people welcomed Pike and took care of him and his men, feeding them and providing them shelter.

Pike's Lost Papers Found

In the early 1900s, historian Herbert Bolton found some of Pike's papers that were confiscated by the Spanish. This important discovery helped fill in some of the missing pieces of Pike's story. Pike's papers are now in the National Archives in Washington DC.

Women from the villages tended to the men's frostbitten feet. They were not treated like prisoners. Rather, they were treated like guests. People played music, sang, and danced with the U.S. soldiers.

PIKE'S OBSERVATIONS

As he passed through each village, Pike made note of the location, population, and character of its people. He observed buildings, houses, water sources, and military units and took every opportunity to speak with townspeople. His Spanish escorts were extremely lenient. They let him go wherever he wanted, and they did not watch him closely.

While Pike was making his observations, he was aware that the settlers were observing him as well. He was embarrassed about the way he and his men looked. They did not have proper boots or hats, and their clothes were torn to shreds. They had

Prison Buddies

In San Juan, New Mexico, Pike encountered a French trader named Baptiste La Lande. He approached Pike and said, "My friend, I am very sorry to see you here: we are all prisoners in this country and can never return. I have been a prisoner for nearly three years and cannot get out."[1]

Pike did not seem worried by this information. "I feel no apprehension," he said, despite the fact that he was a prisoner, too.[2] Pike was confident that his status as a U.S. Army officer and his abilities as a negotiator would eventually ensure his return home.

scraggy beards and long, unruly hair. Pike wanted to make a good impression on the Spanish, but he was barely recognizable as a U.S. soldier. He asked his Spanish escorts if he could borrow some clothing.

SANTA FE

After traveling for about a week, Pike and his escorts arrived in Santa Fe. The governor of New Mexico, Juan de Real Alencaster, greeted him with angry accusations. Alencaster and Pike exchanged the following words:

> [Alencaster]: You come to reconnoiter [explore] our country, do you?

> Pike: I marched to reconnoiter our own.

> [Alencaster]: In what character are you?

> Pike: In my proper character, as an officer of the United States Army.[3]

Despite Pike's denials, Alencaster remained suspicious. Nonetheless, he released Pike and his men into Santa Fe. He allowed the men to talk with the people, but they were followed everywhere they went. Rumors spread that Pike's arrival was the first wave of an invasion attempt by Wilkinson. The

The people of Santa Fe provided Pike and his men with food and shelter.

Spanish worried that a larger, better-armed force
was approaching their borders.

Paranoid about a U.S. military invasion, the
Spanish treated Pike and his men well. They did not
want to give the United States any reason to attack.

They gave Pike all the food, clothing, and shelter he and his men needed, and they were allowed to keep their guns. The Spanish did confiscate some of Pike's papers, however, telling him that he could no longer take notes. Regardless, Pike secretly continued his journaling. He hid the papers in the barrels of his men's guns, intending to smuggle them back to the United States.

CHIHUAHUA TO NATCHITOCHES

The Spanish soon led Pike and his men out of Santa Fe toward Chihuahua. They planned to escort them all the way back to the United States, taking them to Natchitoches, a city located near the boundary of the Louisiana Purchase, in the present-day state of Louisiana. On their journey southward, they passed through the then-Spanish cities of Albuquerque and El Paso.

Prisoners Until Death

Not all of Pike's men were released with him at Natchitoches. Five of his men were held as prisoners in New Spain for five more years.

While imprisoned, Sergeant William Meek and Private Theodore Miller got into a fight. Meek ended up killing Miller. For his crime, Meek was held in New Spain much longer than the others. He was not released until 1821, 14 years after Pike and his men had arrived at Natchitoches.

At Chihuahua, Pike met with Governor Nemesio Salcedo. Salcedo was a very powerful man who believed it was his duty to halt the westward expansion of the United States by any means necessary. He had been successful in blocking two previous U.S. expeditions along the Red River, and he had also attempted to intercept the Lewis and Clark expedition. He did not trust General Wilkinson, who he knew to be a double agent, traitor, and spy. Needless to say, the governor was just as curious about Pike's presence in his area as the rest of the Spanish had been. He believed Pike, too, was a spy and demanded an explanation from the United States. President Jefferson

An Angry King

The king of Spain was furious with Governor Alencaster when he learned what had happened with Pike. He was angry for several reasons. First, Alencaster had brought a suspected spy from the New Spain border into Santa Fe. Second, Alencaster sent Pike even deeper into the heart of the country to Chihuahua, something Pike never could have done on his own. The governor had accidentally helped Pike's mission. Alencaster also decided to release Pike back into the United States before Spain received any apology or explanation from the U.S. government. The king felt Alencaster had committed some very serious errors in judgment, and he removed him from office. The king also reprimanded Governor Salcedo for releasing Pike before getting an apology from the United States.

It was quite fortunate for Pike and his men that they managed to get out of New Spain when they did. If the king had had his way, the explorers might have been held much longer.

defended Pike's trip and denied that he was a spy. Salcedo held Pike and examined his written orders, but he eventually released him.

The Spanish escorts then led Pike and his men north. On July 1, 1807, they arrived at Natchitoches. Pike and his team were home. ⌣

During their journey home, Pike and his men were escorted by the Spanish through the city of El Paso.

Chapter 8

Aaron Burr, speaking to his followers, 1805

RETURNING HOME

At Natchitoches, Pike and his men were released back into the Louisiana territory. Pike managed to smuggle some of his notes back into the country, thus giving the United States the first written report on Spanish territory. Though the Spanish had treated him kindly, they still believed Pike was guilty of espionage. The Spanish government immediately demanded an apology from the United States for sending a spy into their land.

Secretary of State James Madison wrote a letter to the Spanish, reassuring them that Pike had been assigned to explore the Arkansas and Red rivers. Like President Jefferson did before, Madison denied that Pike was sent to New Spain as a spy. The Spanish leaders did not believe Madison. Upset about Pike's breach of their borders, the Spanish government ended its diplomatic relations with the United States.

AARON BURR'S TREASON

A lot had happened in the United States while Pike was away. In August 1806, one month after Pike left St. Louis, Aaron Burr's plot against Jefferson was uncovered. Burr wrote a letter to General Wilkinson, telling him their plan was about to be put into action. At the time, Burr was in Ohio, on his way south to New Orleans. From there, he planned to invade and conquer Spanish-ruled Mexico. Burr told Wilkinson that his army was preparing to attack and assured him he had the support of the British and the French, as well as a group of Mexicans who wanted liberation from Spain.

Even though this was the moment he had been waiting for, Wilkinson panicked when Burr's letter arrived. Perhaps he realized Burr's plan would not be successful. Or perhaps he lost his nerve. Either way, he changed his mind about his partnership with Burr. Wilkinson immediately wrote to Jefferson, informing him of Burr's treasonous letter. Wilkinson conveniently failed to mention that he, too, had been part of the scheme. He even offered to testify against Burr in court.

Burr was arrested and tried several times in different locations throughout the

A Bear of a Gift

The Spanish seized most of Pike's possessions while he was in New Spain, including the items he was planning to give the president. Hearing that Lewis and Clark had presented Jefferson with live prairie dogs and a magpie from their explorations, Pike wanted to do even better. In New Spain, Pike bought a pair of captured baby grizzly bears. He sent them to the president along with a letter. In the letter, he gave instructions for the bears' care. He also told the president that the bears were quite tame. He claimed they had been raised by humans and would not harm anyone.

Jefferson kept the bears for a short time before sending them to his friend Charles Willson Peale, who owned a museum and zoo in Philadelphia. As they grew, they became unmanageable. The cage Peale kept them in was not strong enough to hold the full-grown bears. One of them escaped and terrorized Peale's family. Peale shot and killed both bears.

country. The charges against him included treason against the United States and conspiring to attack a neighboring nation during peacetime. Burr managed to escape conviction at each trial. Even the Supreme Court justices found him not guilty. There simply was not enough evidence to convict Burr of treason.

WILKINSON UNMASKED

Wilkinson thought himself to be quite clever by betraying Burr while managing to save himself. He was wrong. Wilkinson's role in the scheme soon came to light. Instead of being tried in a federal or state court, Wilkinson was tried in a court martial, which is a trial conducted within the U.S. military. At the time, Wilkinson was allowed to select his own jury from among his fellow officers. Naturally, he chose officers who liked him or owed him favors. He was found not guilty, and he kept his post as General of the U.S. Army.

PIKE UNDER SUSPICION

Pike returned from his travels expecting a grand celebration in his honor. Instead, he was accused of conspiring with Wilkinson and Burr. The fact that he had been captured by Spanish authorities for conducting an illegal expedition did not help his image. Nor did the fact that he was followed home by harsh letters from the Spanish leaders, demanding an apology from the U.S. government for an invasion they had not authorized.

This air of suspicion contributes to the reason why Pike is not as celebrated as his contemporaries, Lewis and Clark. To this day, no one is sure how much Pike knew about the Wilkinson-Burr conspiracy.

First Eyewitness Account

In September 1807, Pike moved his family to Washington DC. He worked to get his expedition journals published. He met with Jefferson in an effort to clear his name from being associated with the Wilkinson-Burr scandal. It did not work.

AN ACCOUNT OF EXPEDITIONS

TO THE

Sources of the Mississippi,

AND THROUGH THE

WESTERN PARTS OF LOUISIANA,

TO THE SOURCES OF THE

ARKANSAW, KANS, LA PLATTE, AND PIERRE
JAUN, RIVERS;

PERFORMED BY ORDER OF THE

GOVERNMENT OF THE UNITED STATES

DURING THE YEARS 1805, 1806, AND 1807.

AND A TOUR THROUGH

THE

INTERIOR PARTS OF NEW SPAIN,

WHEN CONDUCTED THROUGH THESE PROVINCES,

BY ORDER OF

THE CAPTAIN-GENERAL,

IN THE YEAR 1807.

BY MAJOR Z. M. PIKE.

ILLUSTRATED BY MAPS AND CHARTS.

PHILADELPHIA:

PUBLISHED BY C. & A. CONRAD, & Co. No. 30, CHESNUT STREET. SOMER-
VELL & CONRAD, PETERSBURGH. BONSAL, CONRAD, & Co. NORFOLK.
AND FIELDING LUCAS, Jr. BALTIMORE.

John Binns, Printer....1810.

Pike's memoirs

Pike's journals, *An Account of Expeditions to the Sources of the Mississippi* and *Through the Western Parts of Louisiana*, were published in 1810. The journals were the first recorded eyewitness accounts of Spanish settlements, and his observations turned out to be an important resource for the United States. Pike's notes recorded previously unknown details about daily life in these settlements, the Spanish military, and the region's natural resources.

Pike's journals inspired some U.S. traders to venture to Santa Fe for business. At first, the Spanish governors did not want to trade with the United States. But after Mexican Independence in 1821 ended Spanish authority in Mexico, a system of trade was eventually established in the Southwest. This may have been the only successful piece of Wilkinson's plot, though he never benefited from the business as he had hoped.

WAR OF 1812

In 1812, the United States again went to war with Great Britain. The United States had already won its independence. This time, Britain's presence in Canada and its control over trade in Europe was at issue.

Eager to restore his good name, Pike volunteered to take a command. The U.S. military struggled and was

First Account

Pike's journals were printed by Joseph Binns, the man responsible for printing the United States Constitution. The journals' publication did not erase the hints of scandal surrounding Pike, but they were well received. Pike's journals were published before those of Lewis and Clark, and they gave the first account of the West to a public that was eager to learn about the new territory.

often forced to retreat when faced by the British. However, Pike proved to be a good leader and was soon promoted to general.

In April 1813, Pike was given command of a 1,700-man troop and led the successful attack on York, the present-day Canadian city of Toronto. He and his men ferried across Lake Ontario and attacked the 800 British soldiers who were guarding the important storehouses and government buildings. The British retreated, but this was because the British commander had a plan. The commander had constructed a large explosive mine, and he wanted to lure the U.S. soldiers off the beach and onto the hidden mine, eventually setting it off. However, the mine was set off too early, sending debris flying in all directions. Pike, from a raised section of land, was watching the British soldiers retreat and enjoying the first victory of his military career,

Pike Honored

Pike was nationally recognized for his military contributions in the War of 1812. The Battle of York was the first significant U.S. victory in the conflict. President James Madison honored Pike posthumously by having a new battleship named in his honor—the General Pike.

when he was hit in the back by a large rock thrown up from the explosion. He died as a result of his injuries, on April 27, 1813, at the age of 34. ⌐

Costly Error

The British commander who set off the mine explosion too early made several fatal mistakes that day. Not only did the explosion take Pike's life and the lives of 52 other U.S. soldiers, it killed 42 of the commander's own British soldiers as well. It wounded 180 others.

One of the last battles of the War of 1812, the battle of New Orleans

Zebulon Pike and other expedition members looking at a mountain peak in the Rockies.

UNDERSTANDING PIKE

uring his expeditions, Pike made many odd decisions that resulted in almost as many mistakes. The scholars and historians who study his life and travels do not always agree on why he made the choices he made. Was Pike a young, inexperienced explorer who was not equipped to complete the difficult tasks that were assigned to him? Or was he a pawn in General Wilkinson's scheme? Evidence supports both theories.

PIKE WAS INEXPERIENCED

It is clear that Pike really believed he was one of the great explorers of the western frontier. He received a clear set of orders from Wilkinson, and he did his best to follow them carefully. He took his responsibilities quite seriously. He drew maps of the areas he and his team traveled. He wrote many pages of notes about his negotiations with the Native Americans. Pike also wrote about himself in a favorable manner. He truly thought he was a magnificent adventurer, despite the fact that he was often confused and lost during his journeys. But it does not seem

No Reward

After Pike returned home from his journey and moved to Washington, Pike approached President Jefferson for additional payment for his services. Pike was paid as a soldier, not as an explorer. Jefferson refused, for he considered Pike part of Burr's conspiracy. Pike persisted. He wanted to be honored, as were Lewis and Clark, who upon their return had been given money and grants of land. Pike was never awarded any additional rewards from the government.

reasonable to suspect that he purposely misled his team.

Pike never admitted to knowing about the Wilkinson-Burr plot. He returned from Mexico expecting a joyful celebration of his efforts. Instead, he found himself in the middle of a political scandal. He worked hard to clear his name of any association with the scandal. He was heartbroken that he did not receive any praise for his hard work. Pike very well could have been a simpleminded, well-intended soldier who made decisions without fully thinking them through.

Pike Was a Pawn

At many points along his journey, it appears that Pike had two sets of orders from Wilkinson. The public set of orders instructed him to communicate with the Native American tribes and explore the headwaters of the southwestern rivers. The other set instructed Pike to make his way into New Spain and take notes on his observations. Pike wanted to prove himself to Wilkinson. Therefore, it is believable that Pike, being the loyal soldier he was, followed all of the general's orders without knowing or questioning why.

PIKE'S MISTAKES

Theories aside, Pike made many strange decisions during his journeys. He led his men into winter weather wearing summer uniforms. He also made them travel through harsh winter snows even when they had the opportunity to wait them out in shelter. It is not clear why he did that. A possible explanation is that by January, Pike and his men were running short on supplies and had nowhere to turn for more. Perhaps Pike did not think that staying where they were—even if they did have a

Another Theory: Espionage

Some historians and scholars believe Pike was a full-fledged spy. They doubt that Pike was an inexperienced explorer who was prone to getting lost. They also doubt that Pike was a mere player in General Wilkinson's plot. Rather, they believe that Pike knew all along what Wilkinson was planning and that he was an active participant. Although enough counterevidence exists to refute this theory, there is no doubt that the following men were guilty of espionage:

- John Andre, a messenger and aide to a British general, conspired with Benedict Arnold to capture the fort of West Point.
- Benedict Arnold was a spy for the British during the American Revolution.
- Belle Boyd, a spy for the Confederate Army during the Civil War, used secret codes to inform the Confederates about Union Army activities.
- Whittaker Chambers, originally a spy for the Soviet Union during the Cold War, switched sides and spied for the United States.
- Robert Hanssen, a CIA agent, secretly passed classified information to the Russian government.

shelter to protect them from the cold—was a good alternative. They eventually would have run out of supplies. Perhaps Pike's own physical strength and resistance to cold prevented him from realizing how much his men were suffering. This was one of Pike's particularly tragic decisions—several men lost their toes and feet because of Pike's stubbornness.

Pike's other major mistake was getting lost several times. First he became lost in the Rocky Mountains, then later in the Sangre de Cristo Mountains. Pike was nowhere near the Red River where he was supposed to be. He wandered in a large circle for a month. He hunted for the trail of the Spanish riders, even though he knew it took him in the opposite direction of his expedition route. However, when he and his team were captured by the Spanish, it actually helped him get to Santa Fe, exactly where he wanted to go. So perhaps getting lost was not a mistake after all. Perhaps Pike intentionally led his team in the wrong direction.

It is unclear whether Pike was an inexperienced explorer or a pawn in

Zebulon Pike Memorial Plaza

Many people today believe Pike's expedition is worthy of celebration. In 2006, to honor the 200th anniversary of Pike's journey, a special park was built in Larned, Kansas. The park is called Zebulon Pike Memorial Plaza. It was dedicated on October 29, 2006, the day Pike passed through the area.

The commemorative coin made for the bicentennial of the Pike Expedition

Wilkinson's plot. Pike's thoughts, motivations, and decisions will continue to be debated by historians. In some ways, Pike's expedition may be less significant for what it actually accomplished than for what it almost caused.

Pike's wandering caused a diplomatic crisis that easily could have escalated into a full-fledged

Pikes Peak

The discovery of Pikes Peak is certainly the major part of Pike's legacy. Strangely enough, he never climbed the mountain that is named for him. Regardless, Pike's hike into the foothills below Pikes Peak was the first high-altitude mountain climbing attempt ever made by a U.S. explorer in the Rockies.

Doctor Edwin James became the first person in recorded history to climb the Grand Peak that Pike made note of in his journals. James climbed the mountain in 1820 with two other men who were part of a Rocky Mountains exploration led by Major Stephen H. Long. In recognition of their efforts, Long called the mountain James Peak.

The first effort to name the mountain after Pike occurred in 1818, in a map created by Doctor Robinson. The peak was officially named after Zebulon Pike in 1843 or 1844 when John C. Frémont explored the area.

war with Spain. However, Pike's contributions—his published observations of New Spain and his firsthand investigation of the southwest extreme of U.S. territory— are undeniable. Pike proved himself after his travels as well, turning out to be a strong leader during the War of 1812. He charged onto his final battlefield with his head high, and he left it tasting victory. These are small achievements in the great landscape of history, but even such seemingly insignificant actions on the part of individuals can shape a nation.

Pikes Peak

TIMELINE

1779

Zebulon Pike is born in Lamberton, New Jersey, on January 5.

1792

Pike's family moves to Fort Washington, where he meets General James Wilkinson.

1794

Pike enlists in the U.S. Army.

1805

On September 23, Pike purchases a plot of land from the Sioux, which becomes Fort Snelling.

1806

On February 1, Pike arrives at Leech Lake, which he incorrectly identifies as the headwaters of the Mississippi River.

1806

Pike returns to St. Louis on April 30.

1803

1805

1805

The Louisiana Purchase treaty is signed in Paris on May 2.

General Wilkinson secretly meets with Aaron Burr in June to plot against the United States.

The first Pike expedition begins on August 9.

1806

1806

1806

The second Pike expedition begins on July 15.

Pike arrives at the Pawnee village on September 25, and White Wolf tells him the Spanish are looking for him.

On October 8, General Wilkinson betrays his coconspirator, exposing Vice President Aaron Burr's treason.

TIMELINE

1806

Pike sees the Grand Peak, later named Pikes Peak, for the first time on November 15.

1807

Spanish dragoons arrive at Pike's fort on the Rio Conejos on February 26.

1807

Pike is released into Natchitoches, Louisiana, on July 1.

1810

Pike's journals are published.

1807

Pike reaches Santa Fe on March 3 and meets with Governor Juan de Real Alencaster.

1807

Pike reaches Chihuahua on April 2, and he meets with Governor Nemesio Salcedo.

1812

On June 18, the United States declares war on Great Britain (War of 1812).

1813

Pike dies at the Battle of York on April 27.

ESSENTIAL FACTS

DATE OF EVENT

August 1805–July 1807

PLACE OF EVENT

Mississippi River, southwest region of the Louisiana Purchase territory, New Spain

KEY PLAYERS

* ❖ Zebulon Montgomery Pike (U.S. Army lieutenant and explorer)
* ❖ Thomas Jefferson (U.S. president)
* ❖ James Wilkinson (U.S. Army general and schemer)
* ❖ Aaron Burr (U.S. vice president)
* ❖ Doctor John Robinson (physician and agent of General Wilkinson)
* ❖ White Wolf (Pawnee chief)
* ❖ Juan de Real Alencaster (Santa Fe governor)
* ❖ Nemesio Salcedo (Chihuahua governor)

Highlights of Event

❖ In 1805, General James Wilkinson commissioned Zebulon Montgomery Pike to conduct his first expedition to find the source of the Mississippi River.

❖ In 1806, Wilkinson commissioned Pike to conduct a second expedition to reach the Spanish-ruled city of Santa Fe and record observations of the Spanish settlers.

❖ In 1807, Pike returned home from his second expedition and was accused of conspiring with Burr and Wilkinson.

❖ In 1810, Pike published his journals, which were the first ever recorded eyewitness accounts of Spanish settlements in New Mexico.

❖ In 1813, Pike served as a general in the Battle of York during the War of 1812, and he later died due to injuries resulting from a gunpowder explosion.

Quote

"Nothing that Zebulon Montgomery Pike ever tried to do was easy, and most of his luck was bad."—*Donald Jackson*, The Journals of Zebulon Montgomery Pike

ADDITIONAL RESOURCES

SELECT BIBLIOGRAPHY

Blevins, Tim, et al, Ed. *To Spare No Pains: Zebulon Montgomery Pike and His 1806–1807 Southwestern Expedition*. Colorado Springs, Colorado: Pikes Peak Library District, 2007.

Coues, Elliot, Ed. *The Expeditions of Zebulon Montgomery Pike*. New York: Dover, 1987.

Hollon, W. Eugene. *The Lost Pathfinder: Zebulon Montgomery Pike*. Norman, Oklahoma: University of Oklahoma Press, 1949.

Jackson, Donald, Ed. *The Journals of Zebulon Montgomery Pike*. Norman, Oklahoma: University of Oklahoma, 1966.

Montgomery, M.R. *Jefferson and the Gun-Men: How the West was Almost Lost*. New York: Crown, 2000.

FURTHER READING

Calvert, Patricia. *Zebulon Pike: Lost in the Rockies*. New York: Benchmark Books, 2005.

Sinnott, Susan. *Zebulon Pike*. Chicago: Children's Press, 1990.

WEB LINKS

To learn more about the Zebulon Pike Expedition, visit ABDO Publishing Company online at **www.abdopublishing.com**. Web sites about the Zebulon Pike Expedition are featured on our Book Links page. These links are routinely monitored and updated to provide the most current information available.

Places to Visit

Jefferson National Expansion Memorial
11 N. 4th Street, St. Louis, MO 63102
314-655-1700
www.nps.gov/jeff/index.htm
This national park, located on the bank of the Mississippi River, includes the Museum of the Westward Expansion and the Gateway Arch.

Pikes Peak
Colorado Springs, CO 80901
800-318-9505
www.pikespeakcolorado.com
Pikes Peak is a popular tourist attraction. Visitors can hike up the mountain on the Barr Trail, drive up using the Pikes Peak Highway, or ride the cog railway. The summit's elevation is 14,110 feet (4,301 km) above sea level.

Zebulon Pike Memorial Plaza
Larned, KS 67550
www.santafetrailresearch.com/pike/plaza.html
This plaza was dedicated in 2006 to honor the bicentennial (200-year anniversary) of the Zebulon Pike expedition. Throughout the plaza, plaques provide information about Pike's life and explorations.

GLOSSARY

barge
A flat-bottomed boat, usually intended to be pushed or towed, for transporting freight or passengers.

commission
A military assignment.

compass
A magnetic device with an arrow that always points north; it is used for navigation.

confiscate
To seize by or as if by authority.

correspondence
The exchange of letters.

diplomacy
A peaceful attempt at negotiations between political leaders.

dragoon
A specially trained soldier who rides into battle on horseback.

espionage
International spying.

expedition
A journey of exploration, with a purpose of bringing back information.

ford
To cross a river on foot, horseback, or in a wagon without the help of a raft, a bridge, or a boat.

gangrene
> The death of human tissue that occurs when blood flow to a particular body part is cut off.

headwaters
> The source of a river.

intrigue
> A scheme or plot.

moat
> A deep, wide trench, usually filled with water, surrounding a fortress.

party
> A group or band of people with a shared purpose.

pawn
> One who is being manipulated by another person.

posthumous
> Following or occurring after death.

scheme
> A secretive plot.

sentry
> A guard.

tributary
> A smaller river that flows into a larger one.

Source Notes

Chapter 1. Lost

None.

Chapter 2. Mind-set of Exploration

1. M.R. Montgomery. *Jefferson and the Gun-Men: How the West was Almost Lost*. New York: Crown, 2000. 2–3.

Chapter 3. A Challenging Life

1. Donald Jackson, Ed. *The Journals of Zebulon Montgomery Pike: with letters and related documents*. Norman, Oklahoma: University of Oklahoma Press, 1966. Vol. 1, vii.

Chapter 4. The First Expedition

None.

Chapter 5. The Second Expedition

1. Donald Jackson, Ed. *The Journals of Zebulon Montgomery Pike: with letters and related documents*. Norman, Oklahoma: University of Oklahoma Press, 1966. Vol. I, 338–339.
2. Ibid. 290.

Chapter 6. The Winter Campaign

1. Donald Jackson, Ed. *The Journals of Zebulon Montgomery Pike: with letters and related documents*. Norman, Oklahoma: University of Oklahoma Press, 1966. Vol. I, 370.
2. M.R. Montgomery. *Jefferson and the Gun-Men: How the West was Almost Lost*. New York: Crown, 2000. 292–293.

SOURCE NOTES CONTINUED

Chapter 7. Encountering the Spanish
1. Donald Jackson, Ed. *The Journals of Zebulon Montgomery Pike: with letters and related documents*. Norman, Oklahoma: University of Oklahoma Press, 1966. Vol. 1, 388.
2. Ibid.
3. M.R. Montgomery. *Jefferson and the Gun-Men: How the West was Almost Lost*. New York: Crown, 2000. 298.

Chapter 8. Returning Home
1. Donald Jackson, Ed. *The Journals of Zebulon Montgomery Pike: with letters and related documents*. Norman, Oklahoma: University of Oklahoma Press, 1966. Vol. 2, 321.

Chapter 9. Understanding Pike
None.

INDEX

Index Continued

ABOUT THE AUTHOR

Kekla Magoon has a Master of Fine Arts in Writing for Children and Young Adults from Vermont College. Her work includes many different kinds of writing, but she especially enjoys writing historical fiction and non-fiction. When she is not writing books for children, she works with nonprofit organizations and raises funds for youth programs.

PHOTO CREDITS